To order additional copies of this book, contact:
Xlibris Corporation
0800-891-366
www.xlibris.co.nz
Orders@ Xlibris.co.nz

# flower

# fleur

# red

# rouge

# car

# voiture

blue

bleu

# duck

# canard

yellow

jaune

# apple

# pomme

green

vert

# balloon

## ballon

orange

orange

# pig

## cochon

pink

rose

# one chair

**1**

# une chaise

# two shoes

**2**

# deux chaussures

# three balls

**3**

## trois boules

# four cups

**4**

# quatre tasses

# five dogs

**5**

# cinq chiens

# six cats

6

# six chats

seven oranges

7

sept oranges

# eight fish

**8**

# huit poissons

# nine stars

**9**

## neuf étoiles

# ten fingers

10

# dix doigts